9780980885546

The Understanding Heart

Compiled by **LOUISE BACHELDER**, with
Illustrations by **STANLEY CLOUGH**

THE PETER PAUPER PRESS
Mount Vernon, New York

COPYRIGHT
©
1966
BY THE
PETER
PAUPER
PRESS, INC.

If I can stop one heart from breaking,
I shall not live in vain;
If I can ease one life the aching,
Or cool one pain,
Or help one fainting robin
Unto his nest again,
I shall not live in vain.

EMILY DICKINSON

The Understanding Heart

We are all citizens of one world, we are all of one blood. To hate a man because he was born in another country, because he speaks a different language, or because he takes a different view on this subject or that, is a great folly. Desist, I implore you, for we are all equally human. . . . Let us have but one end in view, the welfare of humanity.

JOHANN AMOS COMENIUS

Give us grace and strength to persevere. Give us courage and gaiety and the quiet mind. Spare to us our friends and soften to us our enemies. Give us the strength to encounter that which is to come, that we may be brave in peril, constant in tribulation, temperate in wrath and in all changes of fortune, and down to the gates of death, loyal and loving to one another.

ROBERT LOUIS STEVENSON

When I remember something which I had,
But which is gone, and I must do without,
I sometimes wonder how I can be glad,
Even in cowslip time when hedges sprout;
It makes me sigh to think on it, but yet
My days will not be better days, should
   I forget.
When I remember something promised me,
But which I never had, nor can have now,
Because the promiser we no more see
In countries that accord with mortal vow;
When I remember this I mourn, but yet
My happier days are not the days when
   I forget.

JEAN INGELOW

Quick sensitiveness is inseparable from a ready understanding.

JOSEPH ADDISON

   Two chambers has the heart,
   Wherein dwell Joy and Sorrow;
   When Joy awakes in one,
   Then slumbers Sorrow in the other.
   O Joy, take care!
   Speak softly,
   Lest you awaken Sorrow.

HERMAN NEUMAN

He who has more learning than good deeds is like a tree with many branches but weak roots; the first great storm will throw it to the ground. He whose good works are greater than his knowledge is like a tree with fewer branches but with strong and spreading roots, a tree which all the winds of heaven cannot uproot.

The Talmud

There are three men that all ought to look upon with affection: he that with affection looks at the face of the earth, that is delighted with rational works of art, and that looks lovingly on little children.

Anonymous

Those who have the largest hearts have the soundest understandings; and he is the truest philosopher who can forget himself.

William Hazlitt

Half the joy of life is in little things taken on the run. Let us run if we must — even the sands do that — but let us keep our hearts young and our eyes open that nothing worth our while shall escape us.

Victor Cherbuliez

TRUE love's the gift which God has given
To man alone beneath the heaven:
  It is not fantasy's hot fire,
    Whose wishes, soon as granted, fly;
  It liveth not in fierce desire,
    With dead desire it doth not die;
It is the secret sympathy,
The silver link, the silken tie,
Which heart to heart and mind to mind
In body and in soul can bind.

                      SIR WALTER SCOTT

THE web of our life is of a mingled yarn, good and ill together; our virtues would be proud if our faults whipped them not; and our crimes would despair if they were not cherished by our virtues.

                      WILLIAM SHAKESPEARE

PRIDE may be allowed to this or that degree, else a man cannot keep up his dignity. In gluttony there must be eating, in drunkenness there must be drinking: 'tis not the eating, nor 'tis not the drinking that is to be blamed. So with pride.

                      JOHN SELDEN

LIFT up one hand to heaven and thank your stars if they have given you the proper sense to enable you to appreciate the inconceivably droll situations in which we catch our fellow creatures.

SIR WILLIAM OSLER

IDEALS are like stars; you will not succeed in touching them with your hands. But like the seafaring man on the desert of waters, you choose them as your guides, and following them you will reach your destiny.

CARL SCHURZ

EACH heart is a world. — You find all within yourself that you find without. — To know yourself you have only to set down a true statement of those that ever loved or hated you.

JOHANN KASPER LAVATER

GRIEF is a matter of relativity; the sorrow should be estimated by its proportion to the sorrower; a gash is as painful to one as an amputation to another.

FRANCIS THOMPSON

I ASKED God for strength, that I might achieve
I was made weak, that I might learn humbly
  to obey...

I asked for health, that I might do greater
  things
I was given infirmity, that I might do better
  things...

I asked for riches, that I might be happy
I was given poverty, that I might be wise...

I asked for power, that I might have the praise
  of men
I was given weakness, that I might feel the
  need of God...

I asked for all things, that I might enjoy life
I was given life, that I might enjoy all
  things...

I got nothing that I asked for – but everything
  I had hoped for.

Almost despite myself, my unspoken prayers
  were answered.
I am, among all men, most richly blessed!

ANONYMOUS

WHAT a man *is* contributes much more to his happiness than what he *has*.... What a man is in himself, what accompanies him when he is alone, what no one can give him or take away, is obviously more essential to him than everything he has in the way of possessions, or even what he may be in the eyes of the world.

ARTHUR SCHOPENHAUER

   A CHILD's kiss
Set on thy sighing lips shall make thee glad;
A poor man served by thee shall make thee rich;
A sick man helped by thee shall make thee strong;
Thou shalt be served thyself by every sense
Of service which thou renderest.

ELIZABETH BARRETT BROWNING

GOD conceived the world,—that was poetry;
He formed it, — that was sculpture;
He colored it, — that was painting;
He peopled it with living beings, — that was the grand, divine, eternal drama.

CHARLOTTE CUSHMAN

It is my custom every night, so soon as the candle is out, to run over the words and actions of the past day; and I let nothing escape me, for why should I fear the sight of my errors when I can admonish and forgive myself?

I was a little too hot in such a dispute; my opinion might well have been withheld, for it gave offense and did no good. The thing was true; but all truths are not to be spoken at all times. I would I had held my tongue, for there is no contending, either with fools or with our superiors. I have done ill, but it shall be so no more.

Habit is a cable; we weave a thread of it every day, and at last we can not break it.

HORACE MANN

It is far easier to be wise for others than to be so for oneself.

DUC DE LA ROCHEFOUCAULD

There is much satisfaction in work well done; praise is sweet; but there can be no happiness equal to the joy of finding a heart that understands.

VICTOR ROBINSOLL

Abou Ben Adhem (may his tribe increase!)
Awoke one night from a deep dream of peace,
And saw, within the moonlight in his room,
Making it rich, and like a lily in bloom,
An Angel writing in a book of gold:
Exceeding peace had made Ben Adhem bold,
And to the Presence in the room he said,
"What writest thou?" The Vision raised its head,
And with a look made of all sweet accord
Answered, "The names of those who love the Lord."
"And is mine one?" said Abou. "Nay, not so,"
Replied the Angel. Abou spoke more low,
But cheerly still; and said, "I pray thee, then,
Write me as one that loves his fellow-men."

The Angel wrote, and vanished. The next night
It came again with a great wakening light,
And showed the names whom love of God had blessed,
And, lo! Ben Adhem's name led all the rest!
                                    Leigh Hunt

Happiness is not the end of life; character is.
                                    Henry Ward Beecher

WE NEED some imaginative stimulus, some not impossible ideal such as may shape vague hope, and transform it into effective desire, to carry us year after year, . . . through the routine-work which is so large a part of life.
WALTER PATER

LET me go where'er I will
I hear a sky-born music still:
It sounds from all things old,
It sounds from all things young,
From all that's fair . . .
Peals out a cheerful song.
It is not only in the rose,
It is not only in the bird,
Not only where the rainbow glows,
Nor in the song of woman heard,
But in the darkest, meanest things
There always, always something sings.
'Tis not in the high stars alone,
Nor in the cups of budding flowers,
Nor in the redbreast's mellow tone,
Nor in the bow that smiles in showers,
But in the mud and scum of things
There always, always something sings.
RALPH WALDO EMERSON

I HAVE told you of the man who always put on his spectacles when about to eat cherries, in order that the fruit might look larger and more tempting. In like manner I always make the most of any enjoyments, and, though I do not cast my eyes away from troubles, I pack them into as small a compass as I can for myself, and never let them annoy others.
>   ROBERT SOUTHEY

A LOVING heart is the truest wisdom.
>   CHARLES DICKENS

THE greater man, the greater courtesy.
>   ALFRED, LORD TENNYSON

TALK not of wasted affection, affection never
   was wasted;
If it enrich not the heart of another, its
   waters, returning
Back to their springs, like the rain, shall fill
   them full of refreshment;
That which the fountain sends forth returns
   again to the fountain.
>   HENRY WADSWORTH LONGFELLOW

It is better for you to be free of fear lying upon a pallet, than to have a golden couch and a rich table and be full of trouble.

EPICURUS

A TEACHER who can arouse a feeling for one single good action, for one single good poem, accomplishes more than he who fills our memory with rows on rows of natural objects, classified with name and form.

JOHANN WOLFGANG VON GOETHE

NATURE imitates herself: A grain thrown into good ground brings forth fruit: a principle thrown into a good mind brings forth fruit. Everything is created and conducted by the same Master,—the root, the branch, the fruits, — the principles, the consequences.

BLAISE PASCAL

SENTIMENT is the poetry of the imagination.

ALPHONSE DE LAMARTINE

LEAVE something to wish for, so as not to be miserable from very happiness.

BALTASAR GRACIÁN

WHAT is the best thing for a stream? It is to keep moving. If it stops, it stagnates. So the best thing for a man is that which keeps the currents going — the physical, the moral, and the intellectual currents. . . . The secret of happiness is — something to do; some congenial work. Take away the occupation of all men, and what a wretched world it would be!

Few persons realize how much of their happiness is dependent upon their work, upon the fact that they are kept busy and not left to feed upon themselves. Happiness comes most to persons who seek her least, and think least about it. It is not an object to be sought; it is a state to be induced. It must follow and not lead. It must overtake you, and not you overtake it. How important is health to happiness, yet the best promoter of health is *something to do*.

Blessed is the man who has some congenial work, some occupation in which he can put his heart, and which affords a complete outlet to all the forces there are in him.

JOHN BURROUGHS

To ERR is human.

VICTOR HUGO

He is only advancing in life, whose heart is getting softer, his blood warmer, his brain quicker, and his spirit entering into living peace.

JOHN RUSKIN

Grief can take care of itself, but to get the full value of a joy you must have somebody to divide it with.

MARK TWAIN

The perception of the Comic is a tie of sympathy with other men, a pledge of sanity. We must learn by laughter as well as by tears and terror.

RALPH WALDO EMERSON

An inexhaustible good nature is one of the most precious gifts of heaven, spreading itself like oil over the troubled sea of thought, and keeping the mind smooth and equable in the roughest weather.

WASHINGTON IRVING

It is not death that a man should fear, but he should fear never beginning to live.

MARCUS AURELIUS

THE little troubles and worries of life, so many of which we meet, may be as stumbling blocks in our way, or we may make them stepping-stones to a noble character and to Heaven.

Troubles are often the tools by which God fashions us for better things.

HENRY WARD BEECHER

THE tree which needs two arms to span its girth sprang from the tiniest shoot. Yon tower, nine stories high, rose from a little mound of earth. A journey of a thousand miles began with a single step.

LAO-TSE

GOD gives all men all earth to love,
But since man's heart is small,
Ordains for each one spot should prove
Beloved over all.

RUDYARD KIPLING

To BE seventy years young is sometimes far more cheerful and hopeful than to be forty years old.

OLIVER WENDELL HOLMES

IN THINGS that are tender and unpleasing, it is good to break the ice by some whose words are of less weight, and to reserve the more weighty voice to come in as by chance. . . . I knew one that when he wrote a letter he would put that which was most material in the postscript, as if it had been a by-matter.
FRANCIS BACON

ANTICIPATE charity by preventing poverty; assist the reduced fellowman, either by a considerable gift, or a sum of money, or by teaching him a trade, or by putting him in the way of business, so that he may earn an honest livelihood, and not be forced to the dreadful alternative of holding out his hand for charity. This is the highest step and the summit of charity's golden ladder.
MAIMONIDES

THERE is a politeness of the heart. It is akin to love.
JOHANN WOLFGANG VON GOETHE

PRAYER does not change God, but changes him who prays.
SÖREN KIERKEGAARD

A WONDERFUL fact to reflect upon, that every human creature is constituted to be that profound secret and mystery to every other.
>> CHARLES DICKENS

No SOUL is desolate as long as there is a human being for whom it can feel trust and reverence.
>> GEORGE ELIOT

> Do ALL the good you can,
> By all the means you can,
> In all the ways you can,
> In all the places you can,
> At all the times you can,
> To all the people you can,
> As long as ever you can.
>> JOHN WESLEY

THERE's nothing fair nor beautiful, but takes Something from thee, that makes it beautiful.
>> HENRY WADSWORTH LONGFELLOW

HE IS a wise man who does not grieve for the things which he has not, but rejoices for those which he has.

>> EPICTETUS

IF THERE is righteousness in the heart there will be beauty in the character. If there be beauty in the character, there will be harmony in the home. If there is harmony in the home, there will be order in the nation. When there is order in the nation, there will be peace in the world.

ANONYMOUS

> IT IS not growing like a tree
> In bulk, doth make man better be;
> Or standing long an oak tree, three hundred
>   year,
> To fall a log at last, dry, bald, and sear:
>   A lily of a day
>   Is fairer far in May,
> Although it fall and die that night —
> It was the plant and flower of Light.
> In small proportions we just beauties see,
> And in short measures life may perfect be.

BEN JONSON

IF GOD is thy father, man is thy brother.

ALPHONSE DE LAMARTINE

LIFE is too short to be little.

BENJAMIN DISRAELI

God grant that not only the love of liberty but a thorough knowledge of the rights of man may pervade all the nations of the earth, so that a philosopher may set his foot anywhere on its surface and say: "This is my country."

BENJAMIN FRANKLIN

All things are literally better, lovelier and more beloved for the imperfections which have been divinely appointed, that the law of human life may be Effort, and the law of human judgment, Mercy.

JOHN RUSKIN

Oh Thou who art! Ecclesiastes names thee the Almighty. Maccabees names thee Creator; the Epistle to the Ephesians names thee Liberty . . . the Psalms name thee Wisdom and Truth; John names thee Light; the Book of Kings names thee Lord; Exodus calls thee Providence; Leviticus, Holiness; Esdras, Justice; Creation calls thee God; Man names thee Father; but Solomon names thee Compassion, and that is the most beautiful of all thy names.

VICTOR HUGO

THE best thing to give to your enemy is forgiveness; to an opponent, tolerance; to a friend, your heart; to your child, a good example; to a father, deference; to your mother, conduct that will make her proud of you; to yourself, respect; to all men, charity.

JOHN BALFOUR

CORRECTION does much, but encouragement does more. Encouragement after censure is as the sun after a shower.

JOHANN WOLFGANG VON GOETHE

THERE are two worlds: the world that we can measure with line and rule, and the world that we feel with our hearts and imagination.

LEIGH HUNT

EVERY man, however obscure, however far removed from the general recognition, is one of a group of men impressible for good, and impressible for evil, and it is in the nature of things that he can not really improve himself without in some degree improving other men.

CHARLES DICKENS

Endeavor to be patient in bearing the defects and infirmities of others, of what sort soever they be; for thou thyself also hast many failings which must be borne with by others.

THOMAS À KEMPIS

The only way to speak the truth is to speak lovingly.

HENRY DAVID THOREAU

Temperate temperance is best. Intemperate temperance injures the cause of temperance.

MARK TWAIN

I love little children, and it is not a slight thing when they, who are fresh from God, love us.

CHARLES DICKENS

A man should never be ashamed to own he has been in the wrong, which is but saying in other words, that he is wiser today than he was yesterday.

JONATHAN SWIFT

AN ENLIGHTENED mind is not hoodwinked; it is not shut up in a gloomy prison till it thinks the walls of its own dungeon the limits of the universe, and the reach of its own chain the outer verge of intelligence.
>   HENRY WADSWORTH LONGFELLOW

Look to this day!
For it is life, the very life of life.
In its brief course
Lie all the verities and realities of your
　existence:
　　　　The bliss of growth
　　　　The glory of action
　　　　The splendor of achievement,
For yesterday is but a dream
And tomorrow is only a vision,
But today well lived makes every yesterday
　a dream of happiness
And tomorrow a vision of hope.
Look well, therefore, to this day!
Such is the salutation to the dawn.
>   TRANSLATED FROM THE SANSKRIT

WE CAN scarcely hate any one that we know.
>   WILLIAM HAZLITT

MEN are tattooed with their special beliefs like so many South Sea Islanders; but a real human heart with divine love in it beats with the same glow under all the patterns of all earth's thousand tribes.

OLIVER WENDELL HOLMES

THE chief secret of comfort lies in not suffering trifles to vex one, and in prudently cultivating an undergrowth of small pleasures, since very few great ones, alas! are let on long leases.

WILLIAM SHARP

THOU didst bear unmoved
Blasts of adversity and frosts of fate!
But the first ray of sunshine that falls on thee
Melts thee to tears.

HENRY WADSWORTH LONGFELLOW

A MAN can know nothing of mankind without knowing something of himself. Self-knowledge is the property of that man whose passions have their full play, but who ponders over their results.

BENJAMIN DISRAELI

THE happiness of life is made up of minute fractions – the little soon forgotten charities of a kiss or smile, a kind look, a heartfelt compliment, and the countless infinitesimals of pleasurable and genial feeling.

SAMUEL TAYLOR COLERIDGE

AND when we come to think of it, goodness *is* uneventful. It does not flash, it glows. It is deep, quiet, and very simple. It passes not with oratory, it is commonly foreign to riches, nor does it often sit in the places of the mighty: but may be felt in the touch of a friendly hand or the look of a kindly eye.

DAVID GRAYSON

A GREAT man is he who has not lost the heart of a child.

MENCIUS

CERTAIN thoughts are prayers. There are moments when, whatever be the attitude of the body, the soul is on its knees.

VICTOR HUGO

THE dew of compassion is a tear.

LORD BYRON

HAPPINESS, I have discovered, is nearly always a rebound from hard work. It is one of the follies of men to imagine that they can enjoy mere thought, or emotion, or sentiment! As well try to eat beauty! For happiness must be tricked! She loves to see men at work. She loves sweat, weariness, self-sacrifice. She will be found not in palaces but lurking in cornfields and factories and hovering over littered desks: she crowns the unconscious head of the busy child. If you look up suddenly from hard work, you will see her, — but if you look too long she fades sorrowfully away.

DAVID GRAYSON

GREAT battles are really won before they are actually fought. To control our passions we must govern our habits, and keep watch over ourselves in the small details of every day life.

SIR JOHN LUBBOCK

GOOD manners is the art of making those people easy with whom we converse. Whoever makes the fewest persons uneasy is the best bred in the company.

JONATHAN SWIFT

Conviction brings a silent, indefinable beauty into faces made of the commonest human clay; the devout worshiper at any shrine reflects something of its golden glow, even as the glory of a noble love shines like a sort of light from a woman's face.

Honoré de Balzac

In order that people may be happy in their work, these three things are needed: They must be fit for it: They must not do too much of it: And they must have a sense of success in it.

John Ruskin

Never lose an opportunity of seeing anything that is beautiful, for beauty is God's handwriting — a wayside sacrament. Welcome it in every fair face, in every fair sky, in every flower, and thank God for it as a cup of blessing.

Ralph Waldo Emerson

Before we passionately wish for anything, we should carefully examine the happiness of its possessor.

Duc de La Rochefoucauld

Go PLACIDLY amid the noise and the haste, and remember what peace there may be in silence. As far as possible without surrender be on good terms with all persons. Speak your truth quietly and clearly; and listen to others.

You are a child of the universe no less than the trees and the stars; you have a right to be here.

Therefore be at peace with God, whatever you conceive Him to be, and whatever your labors and aspirations, in the noisy confusion of life, keep peace with your soul. With all its sham, drudgery and broken dreams, it is still a beautiful world.

ANONYMOUS

WHOEVER loves much, does much.

THOMAS À KEMPIS

A MYSTIC bond of brotherhood makes all men one.

THOMAS CARLYLE

IMPARTING knowledge is only lighting other men's candles at our lamp without depriving ourselves of any flame.

JANE PORTER

I will tell you, scholar, I have heard a grave divine say, that God has two dwellings, one in heaven, and the other in a meek and thankful heart.

Izaak Walton

> The kindest and the happiest pair
> Will find occasion to forbear;
> And something, every day they live,
> To pity, and perhaps forgive.

William Cowper

The greatest thing a human soul ever does in the world is to *see* something, and tell what it *saw* in a plain way. Hundreds of people can talk for one who can think, but thousands can think for one who can see. To see clearly is poetry, prophecy, and religion, all in one.

John Ruskin

The greatest comfort of my old age, and that which gives me the highest satisfaction, is the pleasing remembrance of the many benefits and friendly offices I have done to others.

Cato

I LIVE in a constant endeavor to fence against the infirmities of ill health, and other evils of life by mirth; being firmly persuaded that every time a man smiles, — but much more so, when he laughs, that it adds something to this Fragment of Life.
LAURENCE STERNE

EARTH's crammed with heaven,
And every common bush afire with God;
But only he who sees, takes off his shoes;
The rest sit round it and pluck blackberries,
And daub their natural faces unaware
More and more from the first similitude.
ELIZABETH BARRETT BROWNING

IF THE greatest philosopher in the world found himself upon a plank wider than actually necessary, but hanging over a precipice, his imagination would prevail, though his reason convinced him of his safety.
BLAISE PASCAL

TO REGRET deeply is to live afresh.
HENRY DAVID THOREAU

Happiness grows at our own firesides, and is not to be picked in strangers' gardens.
Douglas Jerrold

It is surely better to pardon too much than to condemn too much.
George Eliot

No one is useless in this world who lightens the burden of it to anyone else.
Charles Dickens

Not chance of birth or place has made us friends,
Being oftentimes of different tongues and nations,
But the endeavor for the selfsame ends,
With the same hopes, and fears, and aspirations.
Henry Wadsworth Longfellow

The sublime and the ridiculous are often so nearly related that it is difficult to class them separately. One step above the sublime, makes the ridiculous; and one step above the ridiculous, makes the sublime again.
Thomas Paine

LOVE all God's creation, the whole and every grain of sand in it. Love every leaf, every ray of God's light. Love the animals, love the plants, love everything. If you love everything, you will perceive the divine mystery in things. Once you perceive it, you will begin to comprehend it better every day. And you will come at last to love the whole world with an all-embracing love.

FEODOR DOSTOEVSKI

THE responsibility of tolerance lies with those who have the wider vision.

GEORGE ELIOT

No MAN is wise enough by himself.

PLAUTUS

TACT is a gift; it is likewise a grace. As a gift it may or may not have fallen to our share; as a grace we are bound either to possess or to acquire it.

CHRISTINA G. ROSSETTI

FOR all sad words of tongue or pen,
The saddest are these: "It might have been!"

JOHN GREENLEAF WHITTIER

The consciousness of being loved softens the keenest pang, even at the moment of parting; yea, even the eternal farewell is robbed of half its bitterness when uttered in accents that breathe love to the last sigh.

JOSEPH ADDISON

All ages have said and repeated that one should strive to know one's self. This is a strange demand which no one up to now has measured up to and, strictly considered, no one should. With all his study and effort, man is directed to what is outside, to the world about him, and he is kept busy coming to know this and to master it to the extent that his purposes require.... How can you come to know yourself? Never by thinking; always by doing. Try to do your duty, and you'll know right away what you amount to. And what is your duty? Whatever the day calls for.

JOHANN WOLFGANG VON GOETHE

The story of any one man's real experience finds its startling parallel in that of every one of us.

JAMES RUSSELL LOWELL

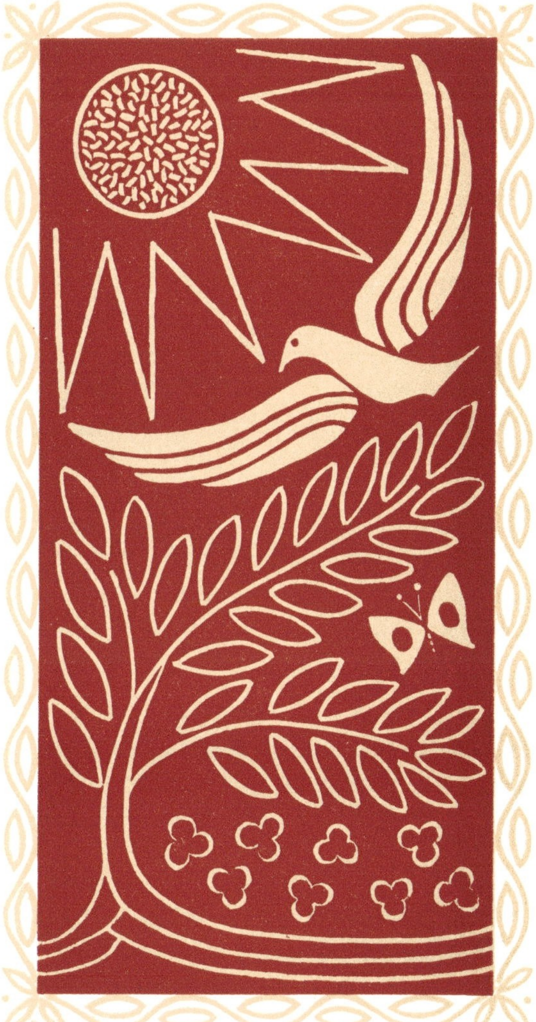

Know you what it is to be a child? It is to be something very different from the man of today. It is to have a spirit yet streaming from the waters of baptism; it is to believe in love, to believe in loveliness, to believe in belief; it is to be so little that the elves can reach to whisper in your ear; it is to turn pumpkins into coaches, and mice into horses, lowness into loftiness and nothing into everything, for each child has its fairy godmother in its soul.
         Francis Thompson

Whenever education and refinement grow away from the common people, they are growing toward selfishness, which is the monster evil of the world. That is true cultivation which gives us sympathy with every form of human life, and enables us to work most successfully for its advancement. Refinement that carries us away from our fellow-men is not God's refinement.
         Henry Ward Beecher

Great perils have this beauty, that they bring to light the fraternity of strangers.
         Victor Hugo

HEAVEN knows we need never be ashamed of our tears, for they are rain upon the blinding dust of earth, overlying our hard hearts.
> CHARLES DICKENS

MORE things are wrought by prayer
Than this world dreams of. Wherefore, let
   thy voice
Rise like a fountain for me night and day.
For what are men better than sheep or goats
That nourish a blind life within the brain,
If, knowing God, they lift not hands of
   prayer
Both for themselves and those who call them
   friends?
> ALFRED, LORD TENNYSON

INTELLIGENCE and courtesy not always are
   combined;
Often in a wooden house, a golden room we
   find.
> HENRY WADSWORTH LONGFELLOW

SOMETIMES it proves the highest understanding not to understand.
> BALTASAR GRACIÁN

QUIET minds can not be perplexed or frightened, but go on in fortune or misfortune at their own private pace, like a clock during a thunderstorm.

ROBERT LOUIS STEVENSON

IT SEEMS to me we can never give up longing and wishing while we are thoroughly alive. There are certain things we feel to be beautiful and good, and we must hunger after them.

GEORGE ELIOT

I DEEM it no less virtue to know how well to keep silence than to know how well to speak; and therefore methinketh that a man ought to have a long neck like a crane so that when a man wished to speak, his words would pass through many joints before they reached his mouth.

ST. FRANCIS OF ASSISI

PITY is often a reflection of our own evils in the ills of others. It is a delicate foresight of the troubles into which we may fall.

DUC DE LA ROCHEFOUCAULD

WHATEVER you do, you need courage. Whatever course you decide upon, there is always someone to tell you, you are wrong. There are always difficulties arising which tempt you to believe that your critics are right. To map out a course of action, and follow it to an end, requires some of the same courage which a soldier needs. Peace has its victories, but it takes brave men to win them.

RALPH WALDO EMERSON

IT IS good to be attracted out of ourselves, to be forced to take a near view of the sufferings, the privations, the efforts, the difficulties of others.

CHARLOTTE BRONTE

THE silkworm weaves its cocoon and stays inside, therefore it is imprisoned; the spider weaves its web and stays outside, therefore it is free.

CHINESE PROVERB

ACTION may not always bring happiness; but there is no happiness without action.

BENJAMIN DISRAELI

A word is not a crystal, transparent and unchanged; it is the skin of a living thought and may vary greatly in color and content according to the circumstances and time in which it is used.
>> Oliver Wendell Holmes

Grief knits two hearts in closer bonds than happiness ever can, and common suffering is a far stronger link than common joy.
>> Alphonse de Lamartine

The best portion of a good man's life, —
His little nameless, unremembered acts
Of kindness and of love.
>> Willam Wordsworth

Very little is needed to make a happy life. It is all within yourself, in your way of thinking.
>> Marcus Aurelius

Those who have suffered much are like those who know many languages; they have learned to understand and to be understood by all.
>> Mme. Swetchine

THERE was never a person who did anything worth doing that did not receive more than he gave.
HENRY WARD BEECHER

TO BE honest, to be kind — to earn a little and to spend a little less, to make upon the whole a family happier for his presence, to renounce when that shall be necessary and not be embittered, to keep a few friends, but these without capitulation — above all, on the same grim condition, to keep friends with himself — here is a task for all that a man has of fortitude and delicacy.
ROBERT LOUIS STEVENSON

JOY is not in things, it is in us.
RICHARD WAGNER

THE thoughts you think will irradiate you as though you are a transparent vase.
MAURICE MAETERLINCK

ONLY watch how the flowers bloom, how the flowers fade; say not this man is right, that man is wrong.
CHINESE PROVERB

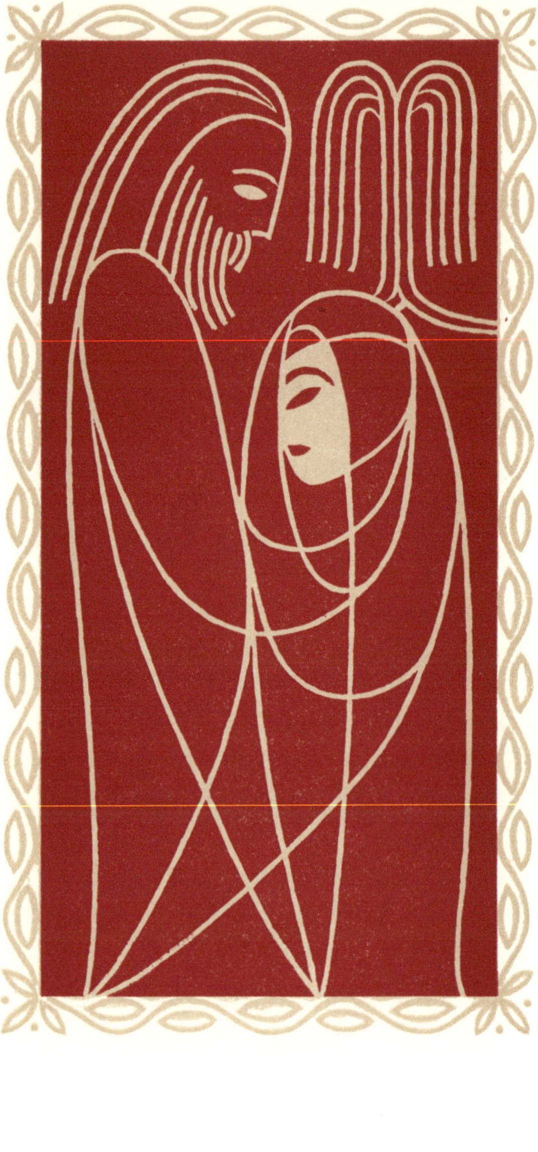

ONE of the most effectual ways of pleasing and of making one's self loved is to be cheerful: joy softens more hearts than tears.
>> MME. DE SARTORY

THE man who cannot wonder, who does not habitually wonder and worship, is but a pair of spectacles behind which there is no eye.
>> THOMAS CARLYLE

THE sense of humor is the just balance of all the faculties of man, the best security against the pride of knowledge and the conceits of the imagination, the strongest inducement to submit with a wise and pious patience to the vicissitudes of human existence.
>> RICHARD MONCKTON MILNES

CONQUER a man who never gives by gifts;
Subdue untruthful men by truthfulness;
Vanquish an angry man by gentleness;
And overcome the evil man by goodness.
>> ANCIENT INDIA

COMPASSION is the basis of all morality.
>> ARTHUR SCHOPENHAUER

PATIENCE serves as a protection against wrongs as clothes do against cold. For if you put on more clothes as the cold increases, it will have no power to hurt you. So in like manner you must grow in patience when you meet with great wrongs, and they will then be powerless to vex your mind.

LEONARDO DA VINCI

You call for faith:
I show you doubt, to prove that faith exists.
The more of doubt, the stronger faith, I say,
If faith o'ercomes doubt.

ROBERT BROWNING

THE grand essentials to happiness in this life are something to do, something to love, and something to hope for.

JOSEPH ADDISON

LIFE is made up, not of great sacrifices or duties, but of little things in which smiles and kindness and small obligations, given habitually, are what win and preserve the heart and secure comfort.

SIR HUMPHREY DAVY

THAT man lives happy and in command of himself, who from day to day can say I have lived. Whether clouds obscure, or the sun illumines the following day, that which is past is beyond recall.

HORACE

SOME of your hurts you have cured,
   And the sharpest you still have survived,
But what torments of grief you endured
   From evils which never arrived!

RALPH WALDO EMERSON

MAN is preeminently a creative animal, predestined to strive consciously for an object and to engage in engineering — that is, incessantly and eternally to make new roads, *wherever they may lead*.

FEODOR DOSTOEVSKI

THERE is a certain relief in change, even though it be from bad to worse; as I have found in traveling in a stage coach, that it is often a comfort to shift one's position and be bruised in a new place.

WASHINGTON IRVING

PERFECTION does not exist; to understand it is the triumph of human intelligence; to expect to possess it is the most dangerous kind of madness.

ALFRED DE MUSSET

POUR out light and truth as God pours sunshine and rain; no longer seek knowledge as the luxury of a few, but dispense it amongst all as the bread of life.

HORACE MANN

GLADNESS can scarcely be a solitary thing. The very life of praise seems choral; it is more than one bounded heart can utter.

DORA GREENWELL

DOING good to others is not a duty. It is a joy, for it increases your own health and happiness.

ZOROASTER

THE ideal man bears the accidents of life with dignity and grace, making the best of circumstances.

ARISTOTLE

You never enjoy the world aright, till the sea itself floweth in your veins, till you are clothed with the heavens, and crowned with the stars: and perceive yourself to be the sole heir of the whole world, and more than so, because men are in it who are every one sole heirs as well as you. Till you can sing and rejoice and delight in God, as misers do in gold, and kings in sceptres, you never enjoy the world.

THOMAS TRAHERNE

Let us not therefore judge one another any more; but judge this rather, that no man put a stumbling block or an occasion to fall in his brother's way.

ROMANS 14:13

Advice is like snow; the softer it falls, the longer it dwells upon, and the deeper it sinks into the mind.

SAMUEL TAYLOR COLERIDGE

All human wisdom is summed up in two words, — wait and hope.

ALEXANDRE DUMAS, *the Elder*

LIFE is short and we have not too much time for gladdening the hearts of those who are traveling the dark way with us. Oh, be swift to love! Make haste to be kind.

HENRI FREDERIC AMIEL

I'LL not willingly offend,
  Nor be easily offended;
What's amiss I'll strive to mend,
  And endure what can't be mended.

ISAAC WATTS

THUS the sum of things is ever being replenished, and mortals live one and all by give and take. Some races wax and others wane, and in a short space the tribes of living things are changed, and like runners, hand on the torch of life.

LUCRETIUS

THE useful may be trusted to further itself, for many produce it and no one can do without it; but the beautiful must be specially encouraged, for few can present it, while yet all have need of it.

JOHANN WOLFGANG VON GOETHE

It is not ignoble to feel that the fuller life which a sad experience has brought us is worth our own personal share of pain. The growth of higher feeling within us is like the growth of faculty, bringing with it a sense of added strength. We can no more wish to return to a narrower sympathy than a painter or a musician can wish to return to his cruder manner, or a philosopher to his less complete formula.

GEORGE ELIOT

At every moment of our lives we should be trying to find out, not in what we differ with other people, but in what we agree with them.

JOHN RUSKIN

There is no greater mistake in the world than the looking upon every sort of nonsense as want of sense.

LEIGH HUNT

You must forgive those who transgress against you before you can look to forgiveness from Above.

THE TALMUD

Happiness is a sunbeam which may pass through a thousand bosoms without losing a particle of its original ray; nay, when it strikes a kindred heart, like the converged light upon a mirror, it reflects itself with redoubled brightness. It is not perfected till it is shared.
Jane Porter

The wealth of a soul is measured by how much it can feel; its poverty by how little.
William R. Alger

To love is the great Amulet that makes this world a garden.
Robert Louis Stevenson

Imagination is the eye of the soul.
Joseph Joubert

He's truly valiant that can wisely suffer
The worst than man can breathe, and make
   his wrongs
His outside, to wear them like his raiment,
   carelessly,
And ne'er prefer his injuries to his heart,
To bring it into danger.
William Shakespeare

Faith marches at the head of the army of progress. — It is found beside the most refined life, the freest government, the profoundest philosophy, the noblest poetry, the purest humanity.

Theodore T. Munger

The supreme happiness of life is the conviction that we are loved; loved for ourselves, or rather loved in spite of ourselves.

Victor Hugo

No great thing is created suddenly any more than a bunch of grapes or a fig. If you tell me that you desire a fig, I answer you that there must be time. Let it first blossom, then bear fruit, then ripen.

Epictetus

A noble heart, like the sun, showeth its greatest countenance in its lowest estate.

Sir Philip Sidney

With mirth and laughter let old wrinkles come.

William Shakespeare

WHENEVER evil befalls us, we ought to ask ourselves, after the first suffering, how we can turn it into good. So shall we take occasion, from one bitter root, to raise perhaps many flowers.
LEIGH HUNT

SURELY it is not true blessedness to be free from sorrow while there is sorrow and sin in the world; sorrow is then a part of love, and love does not seek to throw it off.
GEORGE ELIOT

NEW opinions are always suspected, and usually opposed, without any other reason but because they are not already common.
JOHN LOCKE

TO JUDGE human nature rightly, a man may sometimes have a very small experience, provided he has a very large heart.
EDWARD ROBERT BULWER-LYTTON

A MAN has generally the good or ill qualities which he attributes to mankind.
WILLIAM SHENSTONE

Experience never misleads, what you are misled by is only your judgment, and this misleads you by anticipating results from experience of a kind that is not produced by your experiments.

Leonardo da Vinci

If we could read the secret history of our enemies, we should find in each man's life sorrow and suffering enough to disarm all hostility.

Henry Wadsworth Longfellow

It is not written, blessed is he that *feedeth* the poor, but he that *considereth* the poor. A little thought and a little kindness are often worth more than a great deal of money.

John Ruskin

Who is narrow of vision cannot be bighearted; who is narrow of spirit cannot take long, easy strides.

Chinese Proverb

Trouble that is easily recognized is half-cured.

St. Francis de Sales

I HOLD myself indebted to any one from whose enlightened understanding another ray of knowledge communicates to mine. — Really to inform the mind is to correct and enlarge the heart.

JUNIUS

> So MANY gods, so many creeds,
>   So many paths that wind and wind,
> While just the art of being kind
>   Is all the sad world needs.

ELLA WHEELER WILCOX

NEXT to love, sympathy is the divinest passion of the human heart.

EDMUND BURKE

> THOU hast given so much to me,
> Give one thing more — a grateful heart;
> Not thankful when it pleaseth me,
> As if Thy blessings had spare days,
> But such a heart whose pulse may be
> Thy praise.

GEORGE HERBERT

THE more a man knows, the more he forgives.

ANONYMOUS